10 Ways To Make Time Work For You

Jimmy D. Bayes, Ph.D.

10 WAYS TO MAKE TIME WORK FOR YOU

Copyright © 2018 Dunamis Publications
A Service of Dunamis Empowerment Foundation
Bryan, Texas 77808

ISBN: 0996582444
ISBN-13: 978-0996582445

No part of this publication may be produced, stored in a retrieval system or transmitted in any form or by any means, electronic, mechanical, photocopying, recording, scanning, or otherwise, except as permitted by the U.S, Copyright Act, without either the prior written or electronic permission of the author or the controlling authorities of Dunamis Empowerment Foundation.

Communication or requests to the author should be addressed to *director@dunamisempower.org*.

This publication is designed to provide accurate and authoritative information in regard to the subject matter covered. It is provided with the understanding that the author is not responsible for the results that may occur in applying the following information.

Dunamis Publications
Copyright © 2018
All rights reserved.

Dunamis Empowerment Foundation

Dunamis is a 501c3 nonprofit organization established for the purpose of empowering people. In terms of impact, education is the best (but not only) way to empower people. Dunamis Publications is a function of the foundation to give people a voice and to provide material that will inspire and empower.

Go to *www.dunamisempower.org* for more information or to donate a tax deductible gift.

"10 Ways To Make Time Work For You"

CONTENTS

Acknowledgments	i
Introduction	1
#1 Make Goals That Work	5
#2 Prioritize Time	13
#3 Plan Time Wisely	19
#4 Overcome Procrastination	27
#5 Manage a Crisis	33
#6 Create a Workplace That Works	39
#7 Delegate Work	45
#8 Use Rituals	52
#9 Manage Meetings	57
#10 Alternatives to Meetings	63
About the Author	69
Other Books by Author	70

ACKNOWLEDGMENTS

I would like to acknowledge the people that introduced me to time management principles. First, Starla Akers who invited me to a corporate training on time management using the TimeText Time Management System (now Priority Management) and Chuck Redger who provided time management training for staff as the Executive Director at my first job out of college using the Daytimer® System. I would also like to thank Corporate Training Materials.com for providing the outline and case studies.

1
INTRODUCTION

What defines success for you? For me success is being able to do what I want to do with the resources I have. For many people, making lots of money and owning expensive things defines success. Others define success by their happiness and fulfillment in life. I know many that define success in terms of how well they can help people. There are as many views of success as there are people.

Until the last few centuries, people defined life in terms of survival and some parts of the world still do. But most of the world today, defines life in terms of how much power they have and the material possessions they accumulate. Regardless of how you define success and what status you have in life, there is one fact to be sure of—every one of us has the same amount of time each day. How we use that time can be the deciding factor in our success.

10 WAYS TO MAKE TIME WORK FOR YOU is more than another book about time management, it is about understanding the urgency of time and motivating you to make time work for you instead of letting time control your life.

I first learned basic time management principles in my college years. I was invited to participate in a corporate time management seminar in Dallas, TX. Later, in my first job out of college, our director was a huge proponent of time management using the Day-Timer®

system. I have learned one very important thing regarding time management—regardless of the system you use—time management is a tool that you must use to make your life better.

Over the years, I have collected statements about time management which inspire me to be diligent with my time:

- Time management is the act or process of planning and exercising conscious control over the amount of time spent on specific activities, especially to increase effectiveness, efficiency, and productivity.

- Time management is exercising control over your time and not allowing time to control you.

- Time management is optimizing your usage of time to achieve an easier life.

- Time management is a tool consisting of a wide set of rules and personal skills that impact directly on mitigating stress at work and home.

- Time management is the key to high performance levels, productivity, and helps coping with stress and pressure.

- Organizations should treat time management as an essential ingredient to survival.

- Time management skills help to better utilize their scarce time and resources allowing more time to be put on high priority matters which improve job performance and productivity.

The practice of time management, in terms of history, is fairly new, dating back only to the days of the Industrial Revolution in Europe. Prior to the industrial revolution, most people led simple lives as farmers, craftsmen, and the like. Managing time was dependent upon weather and the seasons. The sun and the moon determined time keeping and time management. The industrial revolution brought men and machine indoors to work regardless of the weather. Electricity brought light into the dark of night making "daylight" less significant. The invention of the mechanical clock made it possible to manage time more efficiently.

Stephen Covey (in *First Things First*), identified four generations of time management approaches in use since World War II:

1. First generation was the use of traditional and rudimentary approaches with clock-based reminders and alerts.

2. Second generation was the use of planning and preparation of work schedules and events that included setting time-based goals.

3. Third generation was the prioritization of various tasks and events, and controlling tasks using schedulers.

4. Fourth generation approach to time management is the contemporary approach with aims at prioritizing various tasks and events, but aims at prioritization based on the importance of the task rather than the urgency of the task. This approach focuses on efficient and proactive use of time management.

I am not, however, fond of the term "time management." I prefer to see time as something to partner with, not something to be managed. This approach to managing time is less about techniques than it is a pivot in the way we think about using time.

Time is like having a partner that is skilled at one thing only. Time has only one job. It is to keep the world going at the same pace. It does not matter who you are or where you live, time is no respecter of persons. We each have the exact same amount of time. Our partner time, is dependable. My partner and I can set an appointment two months from now, and my partner insures me that the date will come on time and when expected. Partner time helps me plan for the future and helps me schedule my day.

Time is constant and is a given, but what we can accomplish is not known, constant, or given. There are many variables in the corporate world, but time is a constant. Gravity is a constant for the lumberjack who uses it to his advantage. Because time is a constant, you can use time management techniques to MAKE TIME WORK FOR YOU!

2
#1 MAKE GOALS THAT WORK

Setting goals that work is critical for making time work for you. It is the most important life skill that most people never learn to master.

Setting goals should be done in every area of your life, including finances, your physical body, personal and professional development, relationships, and even your spiritual life. According to Brian Tracy's book, "Goals," fewer than 3% of people have clear, written goals, and a plan for accomplishing them. Learning how to make goals that work puts you ahead of the pack!

Some people blame things that go wrong in their lives on someone or something else. They play the role of the victim and give all of their power and control away. On the other hand, successful people take responsibility for their lives, no matter what the unforeseen events. We should live in the present. The past cannot be changed. The future is the direct result of what you do from NOW on.

A giant step toward achieving your dreams is to set meaningful, long-term goals. Setting and achieving short-term goals will help you accomplish the tasks you need to in order to achieve your long-term goals.

It is also important to make sure that all of your goals are positive, personal, and possible. The "three P's" are powerful aspects of setting goals that work.

Positive

It is difficult to get excited about a goal such as "Find a career that is not boring." Goals should be stated in a positive way so they will make you feel good about yourself and what you will attain. A better way of stating the goal above is "I will enroll in a pre-law class so I can help people with legal problems in the future."

Personal

Goals should be personal. They must reflect your own dreams and values. They should not be the values of the media, people around you, friends, and even your family. When making your goal statement, always use the personal pronoun "I" to brand it as your own. When a goal is personal, you will be more motivated to succeed and take pride in your achievements.

Possible

When you set goals, consider what is possible and what is within your control. Getting into Harvard Business School may be possible if you have exemplary grades, but it is unrealistic if your grades are subpar. In this case, a more reasonable goal would be to attend a state college or a trade school that offers classes related to your chosen vocation. You may also pursue volunteer work that would strengthen your college application.

SMART GOALS ARE GOALS THAT WORK

SMART is an acronym for the set of criteria that a goal must have so that it can be achieved.

Specific

Success Coach Jack Canfield stated in his book, "The Success Principles," that vague goals produce vague results. In order to achieve a goal, you must be very clear about what exactly it is you want to achieve. Listing the benefits to your life that result when you achieve your goal, will give you a compelling reason to pursue the goal.

Measurable

It is crucial in accomplishing goals that you are able to track the progress toward the goal. This is why goals need a measuring system. A method of measuring goals helps you to stay on track and become more motived when you see quantifiable progress toward your goal. Instead of saying that you want to be more productive, say what you will do, then set a target amount or percentage that you will reach.

Achievable

Setting huge goals are great, but setting unrealistic goals are discouraging when your effort does not accomplish the goal. A good goal is challenging, but is also realistic enough that it can be accomplished in the given amount of time.

Relevant

Before making goals, you should define your core values

and your purpose and mission in life. These are the ultimate foundational factors that help determine what you want and how to set goals to get there. Goals themselves do not provide satisfaction, but goals that are in harmony with your life purpose has the power to make you happy and fulfilled.

Timed

Goals must be on a time-table with deadlines. Without these, you do not have a compelling reason to start working on them. When a goal has a deadline, your subconscious is working on the goal even if you are not aware of it.

PRIORITIZE YOUR GOALS

Accomplishing challenging goals takes a lot of mental energy. You should not spread your time thin by concentrating on multiple goals at once. Invest your mental energy on the most important goal first. When prioritizing goals, choose a goal that will have the greatest impact on your purpose or mission.

An important aspect of goal setting is not only identifying what you want, but also what you must give up in your life in order to get it. Most people are not willing to make a conscious decision to give up things in their life necessary to achieve their goals. While working on a doctorate, I gave up leisure activities and family time. A sacrifice I was willing to make to accomplish a major life and career goal.

BELIEVE IN YOUR GOALS

You must believe that your goals will help you create the

life that you desire. One of Stephen Covey's "Seven Habits of Highly Effective People" is to begin with the end in mind. This habit stands on the premise that you must be clear about what you desire to accomplish in life and set goals that you believe will get you there. Decide what your ambition in life is, write it down and let it be your Life Mission Statement.

CASE STUDY

Margaret and Rachel were reviewing their mid-year profit and loss statement in June and saw that they were not making enough money.

Rachel decided to set some SMART goals to come up with their goal of increasing profits. They both sat down to set a **specific** goal. After some brainstorming, they decided they needed to increase revenue by 10%.

In order to keep their goal **measurable**, they were to measure their progress weekly. This would also insure their goal was **attainable** by the end of the year. It would also keep their goal **relevant**. They set a deadline for December so that it would be **timed**.

After using SMART goals and milestones, Margaret and Rachel were more confident in the capability of their business to remain viable.

Review

Read the following example of a goal, then answer the questions.

Example

To have more patience and build better relationships with my coworkers, at Friday's meetings, I will greet team members with a smile and compliment them on their work and ask them if there is anything that I can help them with.

Questions

- How is the goal specific?

- How is it measurable?

- How is it achievable?

- How is it relevant?

- How is it timed?

- How could this goal be "smarter"?

Make the following goals SMART:

- I will become department manager.

- I will earn more money.

- I will write a book.

- I will learn a foreign language.

3
#2 PRIORITIZE YOUR TIME

Making time work for you is about more than time management. It is about managing yourself in relation to time. It is about prioritizing and taking charge of life. Making time work for you means changing habits and activities that cause you to waste your valuable time. It means being willing to experiment with different methods and ideas that enable you to find the best ways to make maximum use of your time.

THE 80/20 RULE

The 80/20 rule, also known as Pareto's Principle, states that 80% of your results come from only 20% of your actions. In virtually every aspect of life we find that the 80/20 principle applies. For most people it comes down to analyzing where you spend your time and what you are doing. Do you focus on the 20% of the activities that are most productive or do you focus on the 80% activities that are less productive?

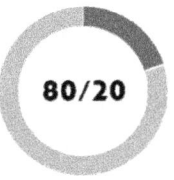

THE URGENT/IMPORTANT MATRIX

Making time work for you means being effective as well as efficient with your time. Having time work for you and achieving the things you want to achieve, means spending time on things that are important and not those things that just seem urgent. This means that you need to be able to distinguish between those things that are urgent and those things that are important.

Important

Activities that lead to achieving your goals and have the greatest impact on life.

Urgent

Activities that demand immediate attention, but are often associated with someone else's goals rather than your own.

This concept has been coined the "Eisenhower Principle." It is said to be how the former WWII General and 34th president of the United States Dwight Eisenhower organized his tasks. Stephen Covey and others seized upon this concept and developed the Urgent/Important Matrix (see below). It is a powerful way of organizing tasks based upon priorities. It helps you to overcome the natural tendency to focus only on urgent activities, so that you will have time to focus on what is important.

IMPORTANT & URGENT	IMPORTANT BUT NOT URGENT
• Crisis • Problems • Deadlines	• Opportunities • Progress • High Value • Long Term
URGENT BUT NOT IMPORTANT	NOT URGENT & NOT IMPORTANT
• Maintenance • Routine Tasks	• Trivia • Entertainment

Important and Urgent

These are activities which relate to dealing with critical issues as they arise and meet significant commitments. →These actives should be done now!

Important, but Not Urgent

These success-oriented activities are critical for you to achieve your overall goals. →You should carefully plan to do these tasks.

Urgent, but Not Important

These activities do not move you forward toward your goals. Manage them by delaying them, cutting them short, or rejecting them. →Postpone these activities.

Not Urgent and Not Important

These trivial activities are usually interruptions and usually just detracts from your goals. They should be avoided if possible. → Avoid them if possible, but *be careful not to mislabel important family and relaxation time as not important.*

BE DECISIVE AND ASSERTIVE

Have you ever had someone make a request of your time that takes away from your important tasks? I am sure that we all have. At times, requests from others may be important and need immediate action. Often, however, requests conflict with our values and takes time away from working on goals that will fulfill our vision and mission. Even if it is something we would like to do but simply do not have the time for, can be very difficult to say no.

If you have the time to help someone and it does not interfere with your important tasks, then you should help. However, many requests pull us away from important tasks and you should say no to these request even though it may be hard to do. One approach in dealing with these types of interruptions is to use a "Positive No," which comes in several forms:

- Say no, with an honest explanation, like "Sorry, I am uncomfortable doing it because…"

- Say no and then clarify your reasoning without making excuses. This helps the listener to understand your position. For example: "I can't do it right now because I have another project that is due by the end of the day."

- Say no, and then give them an alternative. For example: "I am sorry, I don't have time today, but I could schedule it for tomorrow if that works for you."

- Empathetically repeat the request in your own words, and then say no. For example: "I understand you need the paperwork filed today, but I will not be able to do it for you."

- Say yes, but you cannot, give your reason for not doing it, then provide an alternative solution. For example: "Yes, I would love to help you by filing your paperwork, however, I do not have the time today. Can I do it tomorrow?"

- Provide an assertive refusal and repeat it no matter what the person says. This approach may be most appropriate with aggressive or manipulative people and can be an effective strategy to control your emotions. For example, "I understand how you feel, but I cannot file your paperwork for you." Remember to stay focused and not become sidetracked into responding to other issues.

CASE STUDY

Elizabeth was feeling overwhelmed by the huge pile of paperwork scattered on her desk. Her co-worker, Annabelle, told her to sit down and to **prioritize** her work by making two piles of paperwork.

The pile labeled **important** should include items that directly impacted Elizabeth's work performance. The pile labeled **urgent** was to include items that needed attention immediately, however, did not include Elizabeth directly. From these piles, Annabelle told her to create four other piles, in order of importance.

Urgent and important should include items that not only needed immediate attention, but also had a direct impact on Elizabeth.

Important but not urgent should include items that impacted

> Elizabeth directly, but they did NOT need immediate attention.
>
> **Urgent but not important** should include paperwork most likely given to Elizabeth by others.
>
> **Not urgent and not important** were items that were more of a distraction than impactful things.
>
> Thanks to Annabelle's advice, Elizabeth was confident and relieved that she would be able to finish her work on time.

Review

List some real life examples of each category of work:

- Important and Urgent

- Important, but not Urgent

- Urgent, but not Important

- Not Urgent, Not Important

4
#3 PLAN YOUR WORK WISELY

The most important thing that you can do to make time work for you, is being consistently productive every day. Many people use a daily plan to motivate themselves. Having a daily plan and committing to it helps you stay focused on the priorities of that day. Also, you are more likely to get things accomplished if you write down your plans for the day.

START A PRODUCTIVITY PLANNER

Essentially, planning is nothing more than taking a piece of paper and pen and writing down the tasks and the steps that you need to take throughout the day to ensure that your goals are completed.

To start, get a small notebook and label it as your *Personal Productivity Planner* or *Professional Productivity Planner.* You may want to keep two planners so that you can separate work and personal activities.

Label each page with the date and what needs to be done that day. Then prioritize each task in order of importance. Highlight the top three items and focus on those first. Check off the items as they are completed. Items that are not completed can be carried over to the next page.

MAXIMIZE THE POWER OF YOUR PLANNER

Personal development expert, Brian Tracy, believes that

when you write down your action list the night before, your subconscious focuses on that plan while you sleep. By planning the night before, you start fresh and focused on the most important tasks of the day.

Carry your planner with you during the day to avoid becoming sidetracked. Checking off completed tasks will give you a tremendous amount of satisfaction. This helps you maintain your motivation to complete the remaining items on your action list.

Some tasks can only be partially competed. For example, you need to talk with a client. You call him, but only get his voice mail and you leave a message. In spite of your effort, the task is still not finished.

Personally, if I have partially completed tasks at the end of the day, I go ahead and check off the task as finished for that day, but I carry it over to the next day. This way I credit myself for doing what I could, but acknowledge that the task is not complete.

If you find yourself pushing incomplete tasks to the next day, and the day after that, then you need to see how important the task really is and what value it brings. If you postpone a task three times, it may not belong on your list.

THE GLASS JAR METAPHOR

 There is a great story of prioritizing tasks using a glass jar, rocks, pebbles, sand and water to illustrate how to plan your work. The glass jar represents the time you have each day, and each item that goes into the jar represents an activity with a priority relative to its size.

Rocks

Rocks represent the most important tasks to be done each day. The idea is to fill your jar with larger rocks first. Plan each day around the most important tasks that will move you toward your goals. These tasks are of highest priority some with deadlines, *usually important, but not urgent* tasks that move you toward your goals.

Pebbles

After the large rocks, fill the space between the rocks with smaller stones and pebbles. These are tasks that are *urgent, and important*, but contribute less to your overall goal. Without proper planning, these tasks (often unexpected and left unmanaged) can quickly fill your day. Working to reduce these tasks will give you more time to work toward your goals.

Sand

Next, add sand to fill your jar. Schedule *urgent, but not important* tasks only after important tasks. These activities are usually routine or maintenance tasks that do not directly contribute to your goals.

Water

Finally, pour water into the jar. These trivial tasks are usually time-wasters. They are *neither urgent nor important* and take you away from working toward high return activities and your goals.

If you commit to this approach of planning your days, you will see that you are able to achieve more in less time. Instead of finishing things in a mad rush to meet deadlines, each day will be organized and become more productive and profitable.

You will also notice that you spend less time on activities that are of little or no value. Because you have a clear strategy for dealing with competing priorities, stress will diminish, which will allow you to become even more focused and productive.

MANAGING LARGE PROJECTS

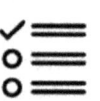

Large projects can sometimes be so overwhelming that it is difficult to plan for them. Chunk, block, tackle is a method of making time work for you that is ideal for taking on large projects. Break down the project into manageable chunks, block off time to work on the project, and then tackle it with a single-minded focus.

Chunk

Break down large projects into specific tasks that can be completed in less than 15 minutes.

Block

Rather than scheduling the entire project all at once, block out set times to complete specific chunks as early in the day as possible. This should allow you to ignore most interruptions and just focus on the task.

Tackle

Now tackle the specific task, focusing only on this task rather than the project as a whole. Completing these tasks gives you a sense of accomplishment by making real progress toward finishing the entire project.

BE PROACTIVE

We have all heard the saying, "Ready, Aim, Fire!" When making time work for you, it is sometimes best to think, "Ready, Fire, Aim" instead. This is because many people aim for the target, then they keep aiming at the target, but they never seem to fire. This is referred to as "failure to launch" and can greatly hinder your success. Some people get so caught up with planning that they fail to take action.

This is just another form of procrastination (discussed in a later chapter). It is usually better to take a shot and see how close you are to the target. Leaders who are decisive, make quick decisions, and act on them are seen as strong leaders even if their decisions are not the best. Sometimes it is best to act quickly with the best information and make adjustments later if needed.

Ready

Do not over-plan each of your actions. By the time you are ready to fire, the target many have moved.

Fire

Remember the 80/20 rule and take decisive action. Even if you do not hit the bull's eye, you will probably be close.

Aim

Evaluate your actions, gain more information, and fire again according to your readjusted aim.

CASE STUDY

John was having trouble figuring exactly what he needed to do in order to optimize his time at the office so that he would not have to bring work home with him. His coworker, Bob, told him to try taking the Chunk, Block, and Tackle approach which would allow him to break up larger projects into smaller and easier to deal with tasks.

The first step for John is to analyze his project and break it up into big **CHUNKS** that could be completed in 15 minutes.

The second step is to **BLOCK** these chunks by level of importance and set a specific time to do them. Ideally, John could begin doing these chunks as soon as he gets to work.

The last step is to **TACKLE** these chunks individually and focus only on them. John could then finish his work at his job and not have to bring any work home.

Review

Personal and professional planners help determine what tasks to prioritize that will produce the greatest results.

- If you use a planner already, explain how you utilize it and how you can improve upon it.

- If you do not use a planner, describe how you can start using one that will be effective.

The Glass Jar Metaphor explains how tasks can be prioritized to accomplish tasks.

- Describe some of the "large rocks" that you are working on to accomplish your goal.

- Describe how your day is filled with "pebble" and "sand" tasks.

- Describe some of the "water tasks" that tend to waste some of your time.

- "Chunk, Block, Tackle" is used to tackle large projects. Describe how you plan for big jobs and how "Chunk, Block, Tackle" might help you.

- Some people are planners and some people are doers. "Ready, Fire, Aim" helps those people who are extreme planners to start projects. Describe how you plan for projects and how "Ready, Fire, Aim" might help you.

5
#4 OVERCOME PROCRASTINATION

Procrastination means delaying a task—or several tasks—that should be a priority. The ability to overcome procrastination and tackle the important tasks which have a large positive impact in your life and work is a hallmark of the most successful people.

WHY WE PROCRASTINATE

It helps to understand why people tend to procrastinate. There are many reasons why we procrastinate. Some are:

- Not having a clear deadline
- Having inadequate resources (time, money, information, etc.)
- Not having a sense of urgency
- Not knowing where to begin
- Feeling of being overwhelmed
- Having a lack of confidence to do the task well
- Procrastinating has become a habit
- Having no passion or adequate motivation for doing the task
- Fearing failure or a negative outcome
- Fearing success

WAYS TO OVERCOME PROCRASTINATION

Your ability to select the most important task at any given moment, and then to start on that task and get it done quickly and efficiently will have the greatest impact on your success than any other quality or skill that can be developed. If you nurture the habit of setting clear priorities and getting important tasks finished quickly, you will find that your time is now working for you.

Here are 10 ways that will help you to overcome procrastination:

1. **Delete it.** Ask yourself what the consequences are of not doing the task at all. Go back to the 80/20 rule—the task at hand may not be important at all.

2. **Delegate it.** If the task isn't important, or if it is not something that you are responsible for doing at all, then maybe the task can be done by someone else.

3. **Do it now.** Postponing an important task that needs to be done only creates anxiety and stress. Doing important tasks early in the day reduces stress.

4. **Ask advice for it.** Asking for advice and help from a mentor, supervisor, or coach can give you some great insight on where to start and the steps for completing a project.

5. **Chop it up.** Break large projects into milestones with actionable steps. As author and motivational teacher, Bob Proctor says, "Break it down into the ridiculous." Huge things don't look as big when you break it down as small as you can.

6. **Obey the fifteen minute rule.** To reduce the temptation to procrastinate, each actionable step for a project should take 15 minutes or less to complete.

7. **Have clear deadlines.** Assign a deadline for project goals and milestones and write them down in your Productivity Planner (p. 19). Make your deadlines known to others for accountability.

8. **Give yourself rewards.** Celebrate the completion of project milestones and reward yourself for getting projects done on time. Celebrating small "wins" will provide positive reinforcement, build self-confidence and self-efficacy, and motivate you toward finishing larger goals.

9. **Remove distractions.** You need to establish a positive working environment that is conducive to getting your work done. Remove anything that you know is distracting to you.

10. **Hire a coach.** In the past ten years, the coaching industry has grown exponentially because people have realized that they can go further and faster with a coach than they can without a coach. Coaches help clarify what you want to accomplish, help you set goals to get there, and provide accountability until you arrive.

"EAT A FROG" METAPHOR

"If the first thing you do each morning was to eat a live frog, then you can go through the day knowing that it is probably the worst thing that is going to happen to you all day long!"

Your "frog" is the task that will have the greatest impact on achieving your goals and the task that you are most likely to procrastinate starting.

Another version of this saying is, *"If you have to eat two frogs, eat the ugliest one first!"*

This is another way of saying that if you have two important tasks to do now, start with the biggest, hardest, the one you are dreading, or the most important task first. Discipline your self to begin immediately and then to persist until the task is complete before you go on to something else. You must resist the temptation to start with the easier task. You must also continually remind yourself that one of the most important decisions you make each day is your choice of what you will do immediately and what you will do later, or postpone indefinitely.

Finally, *"If you must eat a live frog, it does not pay to sit and look at it for a long time!"*

The key to getting time to work for you and reaching high levels of performance and productivity is to develop the lifelong habit of tackling your major tasks first thing each morning. Do not spend excessive time planning what you will do. You must develop the routine of "eating the frog" before you do anything else and without taking too much time to think about it.

People who are effective at making time work for them are those that launch directly into their major tasks, then discipline themselves to work steadily and single-mindedly until the tasks are completed, then plan for the next day's work.

In the business world, you are paid and promoted for achieving specific, measurable results. You are paid for making a valuable contribution that is expected of you. Many employees confuse activity with accomplishment and this causes one of the biggest problems in organizations—poor performance.

CASE STUDY

Jacob had a big problem when it came to procrastination, while his friend Brian was always good to go. One day, Jacob found that his boss had left he and Brian an incredibly large amount of paperwork to do with only a week to do it in. Luckily for Jacob, the level headed Brian was there to help out.

Brian **delegated** half the work to Jacob, and half to himself. Then, he **spit up** the rest into **realistic goals** which made the project less intimidating. After **removing the distractions** around him, Jacob found that not only did they reach their goals on time, but they also had a lot less stress.

After the project was over and all the paperwork was done, Brian decided to treat themselves to coffee at the local Starbucks as a reward for a job well done.

Review

- On a scale of 1 to 10 how do you rate your struggle with procrastination? (One being little and 10 being a lot.)

- Describe an event that procrastination caused you great stress or caused problems.

- How could you have handled the situation above differently? (use the 10 suggestions given p. 28-29)

- What are some of the "frogs" that you need to eat each morning?

- Name other ways that you have overcome procrastination that was not mentioned.

6
#5 MANAGE A CRISIS

You have learned several ways to get time to work for you instead of you working for time.

As you plan better, improve efficiency, and increase productivity, you should encounter fewer crises. But, you cannot plan for every event. Let's look at what to do in a crisis.

WHEN THE STORM HITS

The key to successfully handling a crisis is to move quickly and decisively, but carefully.

The first thing to do when a crisis hits is to identify the point of contact and make them aware of the situation. For this example, we will assume that you are the point of contact.

Next, gather and analyze data.

- What happened?
- What were the direct causes?
- What were the indirect causes?
- What will happen next?
- What could happen next?
- What events or people will this impact?
- Who else needs to know about this?

Every crisis will require different kinds of data, but it is important to take enough time to do thorough, proper research. You do not want to jump into action based on erroneous information and make the bad situation worse.

You will want to identify the threshold time—the time that you have before the situation moves out of your control or becomes exponentially worse. You may also find that the crisis will resolve itself after a certain point of time.

CREATE A PLAN

Once you have gathered the data, it is time to create a plan. The best approach is to:

1. Identify the problem.
2. Decide on a solution.
3. Break it down into parts.
4. Create a timeline.

ACTION PLAN EXAMPLE

<u>Problem</u>: The First Quarter Status Report is overdue.

<u>Solution</u>: Create the First Quarter Status Report.

<u>Timeline</u>: The report must be complete in 48 hours.

ACTION PLAN:

Step	Details	Timeline	Personnel
1	Collect Budget Data	2 hours	Paul S.
2,3	Collect Project Data	3 hours	Me
2,3	Gather Staff Data	1 hour	Me
4	Write Report	8 hours	Me
5	Review/Edit	2 hours	Me
Time		16	

EXECUTING THE PLAN

As you execute the plan, make sure that you continue evaluating to see if the plan is working. In the example above, after looking at the information gathered, you may have realized that you need more details on a particular item. It would be appropriate to add that step and make sure you are still on track for the timeline.

While executing the plan, it is important to keep organized and on top of events to make sure that your plan stays applicable. This will help you deliver accurate, effective communication to others affected by the crisis. In our example, the manager is probably very anxious to get the report.

Lessons Learned

After the crisis is over, take a moment to look at what caused the crisis to happen and how to prevent it in the future. In our example, the Quarter One Status Report was not completed on time. It even sounds like it was not even started altogether. These planning and prioritizing tools should help prevent those kind of emergencies from happening. However, you will likely find that you are always adjusting and perfecting your plan, so it is important to learn from the times when the tools do not work.

You can be prepared for disasters that can't be predicted, such as illness, fire, or theft. In case of an illness, you can prepare a short contingency plan indicating who will be responsible for your correspondence, projects, and general responsibilities in case you are ill for an extended period. Make sure you share these plans with the appropriate people so that they can be prepared as well.

CASE STUDY

Karen was the floor manager of a large paper company. One winter morning, Karen woke up to discover that she had contracted the flu. Karen had to call in sick. Normally, all the duties of the floor manager would fall to the wayside.

Luckily, Karen had been prepared for such a crisis. She had made a plan that would insure that all of her responsibilities were covered.

She also made sure that all the right people were informed and that everyone knew their part in the contingency plan ahead of time.

> When Karen returned to work, she returned with the comforting knowledge that everything ran smoothly in her absence—because she was prepared!

Review

- You just got a phone call that a customer's delivery has not been made and you promised that it would be delivered first thing this morning. What steps would you take to resolve this crisis?

- Your painting crew called you this morning to say that they had a traffic accident. Their truck cannot be driven and they will not make it to the job they were on their way to. You have a contingency plan in place for this type of crisis, what is it?

- You run a small store that sells safety items, gives safety training, and does random drug testing. Your employees are not cross trained and if someone is out, their job is not covered. How can you avoid a crisis?

- At the end of every month, you barely have enough time to finish all of your work. Not finishing all your work each month will lead to a crisis. Working like this is stressful. How can you relieve some of this stress at work?

7
#6 CREATE A WORKSPACE THAT WORKS

For time to work for you effectively and to be productive each day, you should create an appropriate environment. Eliminating clutter, setting up an effective filing system, gathering essential tools, and managing workflow facilitates an effective workplace.

DE-CLUTTER

Removing clutter can be a time-consuming task itself, but a cluttered workspace significantly impairs the ability to find things. You will get the time back that you invest in organizing your workspace—and more! To have the ability to retrieve materials and instruments quickly, you will need an effective filing system that includes three basic kinds of files.

Working Files

Materials used frequently and needed close at hand.

Reference Files

Information needed only occasionally.

Archival Files

Materials seldom used, but must be kept. For ease of retrieval, organize files in the simplest way possible.

Once clutter has been eliminated and other materials have been filed, the effective workspace includes only what is essential: a set of trays to control the workflow on your desk (next topic), standard office supplies, a computer, telephone, and other equipment essential for your job. Everything else, except for what you are working on at that moment, should be kept where it can be retrieved when needed.

MANAGING WORKFLOW

How do you process the mountain of material that collects in your paper and electronic in-baskets? The answer is one message or one e-message at a time.

Many organizational experts believe that the most effective people act on an item the first time it is touched. This can be difficult, but with practice it can become a habit. This is easier done with the 4 D's:

Do it

If an item can be completed in two minutes or less, do it NOW!

Delete it

If the item is trash or junk, delete or trash it. If it is something that you may use later, file it.

Defer it

If the item is one that cannot be completed quickly and is not an important item, then defer it until later.

Delegate it

If a task is not yours to do, then delegate it.

S.T.I.N.G.

STING is an acronym to help you not feel overwhelmed about a task. The steps are:

- **S**elect one task at a time
- **T**ime yourself using a clock for no more than one hour
- **I**gnore everything else during that time
- **N**o breaks until the task is complete
- **G**ive yourself a reward when the time is up

DEALING WITH EMAIL

Electronic communication can be managed just as easily and as quickly as paper using the four D's above. However, there are some more keys that will help you maximize your email time.

- Like other routine tasks (returning phone calls, handling paper mail, checking voice mail), email is best handled in batches at regularly scheduled times of the day.

- Ask your email contacts to use specific subject lines, and make sure to use them yourself. This will help you to determine whether your incoming email is business, personal, urgent, or important.

- Once determining the subject of the message, respond accordingly. Act immediately on urgent and important emails. Personal and non-urgent emails can be read later or during a break.

- Be sure to use your email system to its fullest

potential. There are many email features that are not used. Most email systems allow you to create folders and add keywords or categories to messages that makes information retrieval much easier.

- Many email programs allow you to create rules that automatically move messages to the appropriate folder. This can help you follow an email plan.

- Regularly delete email from your trash can and junk folder.

USING CALENDARS

To manage all of the things that you must do, it is important to organize reminders into a small number of calendars and lists that can be reviewed regularly. A calendar, regular or electronic, is the obvious place to record meetings, appointments, and deadlines.

An annual calendar may be required for those with multiple duties or manage departments. Tasks such as strategic planning, production, human resources, and budgeting require yearly planning. Annual tasks can be broken into monthly tasks which can be seen with a glance at the calendar.

Your Productivity Planner (p. 19) should be used in concert with your calendar. Your planner is a valuable tool for organizing tasks, identifying patterns, improving workflow, and recording work. Your planner is also a historical record of your work.

CASE STUDY

Kevin was very disorganized. His desk was covered with various papers, office supplies, and even a half-eaten doughnut from breakfast the day before. Keven realized that his work was beginning to suffer, so he decided to make a much needed change. He asked a coworker, Bob, if he had any advice.

The first piece of advice was to de-clutter his workspace. Any trash was tossed away, and all of his files were put in the proper place. After that, they made sure it wouldn't happen again by organizing Kevin's work schedule. By tracking his projects and assignments, Kevin could better prepare for them, and wouldn't get overwhelmed again. Now that Kevin is organized, he can now work easily and effectively.

Review

- Describe your workspace.

- What can you do to make your workspace more efficient?

- According to the STING acronym, which do you find most valuable for relieving stress?

- Which of the STING steps do you underutilize?

8
#7 DELEGATE WORK

If you work on your own, there is only so much you can get done, no matter how hard you work. Everyone needs help and support, and there is no shame in asking for assistance. One of the most common ways of overcoming this limitation is to learn how to delegate your work to other people. If you do this well, you can quickly build a strong and successful team of people.

Delegating work can feel like more of a hassle than it's worth. However, when delegating successfully, you can hugely expand the amount of work that you can deliver. When you arrange the workload so that you are working on the tasks that have the highest priority to you, and other people are working on meaningful and challenging assignments, you have a recipe for success.

To delegate effectively, *choose the right tasks to delegate, identify the right people to delegate them to, and delegate in the right way.* There is a lot to this, but you will achieve much more once you are delegating effectively!

WHEN TO DELEGATE

Delegation allows you to make the best use of your time and skills. It helps team members grow and develop and reach their full potential within the organization. Delegation is a win-win situation for all involved when it is done correctly. Keep the following criteria in mind when deciding if the task should be delegated:

- The task should provide an opportunity of growth for the other person.

- Weigh the effort to properly train the other person against how often the task will reoccur.

- Do not jeopardize the success of your project by delegating critical tasks.

- Do not delegate sensitive tasks such as performance reviews or tasks specifically given to you.

When starting out delegating, you may notice that the delegate (person being delegated to) may take longer than you do to complete the tasks. This is because you are the expert in doing the task and the delegate is still learning.

Be patient. If you have chosen the right delegate and you are delegating correctly, you will find that they become more competent and reliable. Delegate to the lowest possible organizational level.

The people who are closest to the work are best suited for the task because they have the most intimate knowledge of the details of everyday work. This also increases workplace efficiency and helps develop people.

TO WHOM SHOULD YOU DELEGATE?

When you have determined a task should be delegated, think about the possible candidates for accepting the task.

Considerations should include:

- What experience, knowledge, skills, and attitude does the person have?

- What training or assistance might they need?

- Do you have the time and resources to provide any training needed?

- What is the individual's preferred work style?

- Do they work well on their own or with teams?

- How much support and motivation will they require?

- How independent are they?

- What are their long-term goals and interests, and do they align with the experience they will be getting?

- What is their current workload and do they have the time to take on more work?

- Will the delegation of this task require reshuffling of other responsibilities and workloads?

HOW YOU SHOULD DELEGATE

Delegation should not be all or nothing. There are several levels of delegation, each with levels of independence and need for supervision.

Examine the image below:

SPHERES OF INFLUENCE

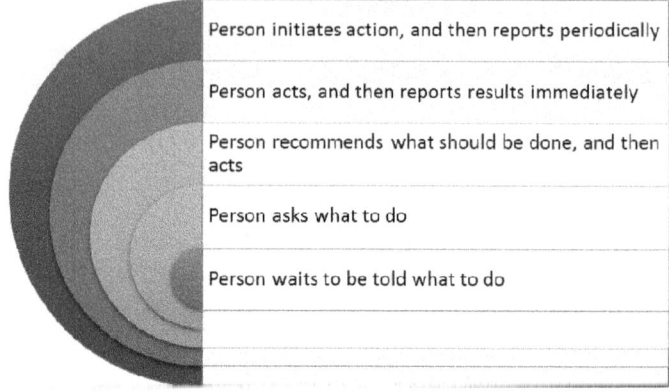

New workers begin in the center—waiting to be told what to do. They work through the spheres as they develop and learn the job until they are able to proactively initiate and complete their work. The point of delegating is not to get people to do your work, but giving others the opportunity to learn and gain experience while helping you complete important tasks.

People move through the spheres depending on their knowledge and experience. You should delegate to people according to the task and to their level of knowledge and skill. Delegate the appropriate amount of authority along with the task, but ultimate accountability always comes back to you.

MAINTAINING CONTROL

Once you have determined the task should be delegated and decided to whom it should be delegated, then brief all team members appropriately. Take the time to explain why they were chosen for the job  and the expectations of the job. Explain the goals, timelines, deadlines, and resources for the project. Work together to make a schedule for updates, milestones, and other key points.

Make sure that the team knows the protocol for dealing with problems or situations that may occur.

Managers should NOT micro-manage. However, this does not mean you set aside your accountability and abdicate all control over the project. When delegating effectively, you have to find the difficult balance between  giving space for people to use their creativity and abilities, while monitoring and giving close support to ensure the job is done correctly.

One method of encouraging growth is asking for recommended solutions when team members come to you with a problem, and helping them explore solutions and reaching decisions.

REVIEW AND GIVE FEEDBACK

All work that is returned to you should be thoroughly reviewed so that the delegate can be given feedback. If possible, only accept good quality, fully completed work. If you accept work that you are not satisfied with, your team does not learn the expectations of the work. Also, if you accept poor work, you may need to complete or redo it.

When good work is returned, make sure that the whole team knows it is good and they get the recognition they deserve. As a leader, you should get in the practice of complimenting members of your team every time you are impressed by what someone has done. Your recognition of them will go a long way toward building their self-confidence and efficacy now and in the future.

> ### *CASE STUDY*
>
> Mary sat at her computer, unable to start the project that Dave had delegated to her. He said that he wanted the chart to only show numbers for this quarter. But did he mean just his sales numbers or the sales number for all of the staff?
>
> Mary was sitting with her email open, weighing the pros and cons of whether or not to send him a message, when a new message came into her inbox.
>
> It was from Dave. "Hi, Mary, I wanted you to know that I'm available to you for any questions or guidance you may need concerning this project. Thanks. Dave."
>
> Mary let out a breath of relief. She wrote back, "Boy, was I glad to see this message. I was just about to ask

> you for clarification."
>
> Dave insured good communication by sending the follow up email to Mary.

Review

- Describe a time that you could have delegated work but did not, and what was the outcome.

- How would the situation been different if you had delegated some of the work?

- When should work NOT be delegated?

- How is delegating different from micromanaging?

- Describe a candidate to whom work should be delegated.

9
#8 USE RITUALS

Ritual is merely formalized behavior or a formal routine, but for many people the word "ritual" conjures up images of boring, repetitive work, with very controlled activities with little room for spontaneity. Ritual and routine, however, can actually help increase spontaneity and fun. Routine tasks are already planned (even scheduled) and you should  have more energy to spend on tasks that will bring you closer to your goals and bring more joy and peace into your lives.

WHAT IS A RITUAL?

The Random House Dictionary defines ritual as any practice or pattern of behavior regularly performed in a set manner.

There are three steps to a build ritual:

1. **Identify the Task.** Starting a exercise ritual for example.

2. **Identify the Time and/or Trigger.** You may prefer to exercise in the morning or evening.

3. **Identify the Sub-Tasks.** Perhaps your ritual involves going to the gym, getting changed, stretching, 45 minutes on the treadmill, three reps of dumbbells, a lap around the pool, and finishing it off with a shower.

A ritual should not be set in stone. Once a ritual is established, it should be modified at any point in time, depending upon your need. In our example, we could easily decide to exercise before work or at lunch and still use the basic task and sub-tasks.

SLEEP, MEALS, AND EXERCISE RITUALS

Everyone should have rituals around their sleep, meals, and exercise for health benefits.

Sleep

Establish a ritual for the 30 minutes before you go to bed. This could include writing in your Productivity Planner for the next day, reading a book, taking a relaxing bath, or doing a bit of yoga. All of these activities will help you wind down and sleep better. It is best to go to bed about the same time each night.

Meals

Taking time on weekends for meal prep or planning helps you eat more nutritiously instead of eating irregularly. Planning each of your meals helps you keep your health goals.

Exercise

Schedule exercise at least three or four times each week for at least 30 minutes. Start with this as a minimum and build upon it.

SAMPLE RITUALS

Here are some rituals that people find helpful making time work for them.

- Instead of checking personal email, news, and social media throughout the day, schedule times during the day to keep tabs. Ritualize this activity by checking email first, then check social media, then other sites of interest without revisiting them again until the next scheduled time.

- Set up a system for maintaining your Productivity Planner. This can be as simple as 20 minutes in the morning to update the day's list, 20 minutes at noon to update what you have done already, and 20 minutes at the end of the day to evaluate the day's activities and plan for tomorrow.

- Perform your tasks in the morning in an organized routine. You can also lay out your clothes and prepare your lunch the night before.

RITUALS MAKE TIME WORK FOR YOU

Once you have used rituals for a while, you may find that you have bits of extra time. For example, you may find that by establishing an exercise ritual, you finish five or 10 minutes earlier because you know exactly what you are going to do at the gym. At the end of the day, you may find that you have 30 minutes unexpected time.

"Triggers" become an important part of ritual. Instead of setting a specific time of day to do a task, choose a situation or event that will cause ritual to come into play.

Examples:

- During lunch or break, read for a development book or check communications.

- Take a few minutes to do deep breathing exercises between tasks.

- Take 5 minutes to clean up your workspace during breaks.

- Take 10 minutes to update your Personal Planner twice or three times daily.

- Set aside one lunch hour a week to do personal errands or make a list at the beginning of each week and do one a day.

CASE STUDY

Linda found that whenever she had a few minutes at work, she would go to check her email. Look at Facebook, and check out new sites. However, while she had planned to only look at these websites for a few minutes, sometimes she would lose track of time. She needed a way to maximize her time without losing track of time on websites and not put her job at risk.

Linda decided to set up several time periods throughout the day when she would check email, her calendar, Facebook, and surf the net. She checked them first thing in the morning, at noon, and at the end of the day. Once Linda got into the ritual of checking these sites only three times a day, she found that she used her time more wisely and accomplished more throughout the day.

Review

- Describe a ritual or two that you currently use that helps time work for you.

- Describe a ritual that will help you get to bed at a good time or that will help you eat or exercise better.

- Describe the frequency and time spent on personal and social media.

- What areas of your time partnership will rituals help you manage time better?

- What are some time wasters that could be eliminated by using rituals?

10
#9 MANAGE MEETINGS

Meetings are often seen as a necessary evil of office life. Few people look forward to meetings—with good reason. Many meetings lack purpose and structure or go too long. With just a few tools, you can make any meeting a much better use of everyone's time.

IS A MEETING NECESSARY?

Deciding if a formal meeting is necessary is the first thing. Perhaps those morning meetings could be reduced to a few times a week instead of every day. Maybe they could take place over morning coffee and be informal or there could be an alternative to having a meeting (the next chapter).

If a formal meeting is called for, you can divide those who attend into two groups; participants and observers. Participants have more seniority, experience, or the subject directly affects their jobs and observers are newer with less responsibility or those not affected directly. Each person should be made aware of their role before the meeting and let the observers choose if they will attend. A follow up report is issued to every employee with the results of the meeting. Participants and observers can be alternated the next meeting if appropriate.

USE THE "PAT" APPROACH

PAT stands for purpose, agenda, and time frame and is a good way to structure meetings:

Purpose: What is the purpose of the meeting?

State the purpose in one short sentence. For example, "This meeting is to review the new invoice signing policy and to decide if a new policy training course is needed." This helps observers evaluate if they need to attend and also help build the agenda and help determine if the meeting was a success by setting a specific goal.

Agenda: This is the backbone of the meeting.

An agenda should be created well in advance of the meeting, sent to all participants and observers, and be used during the meeting to keep things on track.

Time Frame: How long will the meeting run?

Typically, meetings should not exceed one hour. Fifty minutes is better; start 5 minutes after the hour and stop 5 minutes before the next hour. If the meeting needs to be longer, make sure you include breaks or divide the meeting into two or more sessions.

BUILDING AN AGENDA

Before the meeting, make a list of what needs to be discussed, how long you believe it will take, and person who will be presenting the item.

Once the agenda is complete, send it to all participants and observers with the meeting announcement, and preferably two to three days before the meeting. Make sure you ask everyone to sign off on it, and include additions or deletions. If you make changes, send out a single updated copy at least 24 hour before the meeting.

TIME	ITEM	PRESENTER
2:05-2:10	1-Purpose of Meeting	Jill Smith
2:10-2:20	2-Review the current invoice signing process	Joe King
2:20-2:40	3-Discuss New Invoice signing process and need for training	Joe King
2:40-2:50	4-Questions/Answers	Joe king
2:50-2:55	5-Wrap Up	Jill Smith

KEEPING THINGS ON TASK

Note: Formal meetings such as board meetings will require formal protocol and taking of the minutes.

Your job as chairperson is to keep the meeting running according to the agenda. If an item runs past its scheduled time, ask the group if they think more time is needed to discuss the item. If so, how do they want to handle it? They can reduce the time for other items, remove them altogether, schedule an offline follow-up session, schedule another meeting, or allow the meeting to go long. No matter what the group agrees to, make sure that they stick to the decision.

At the end of the meeting, get agreement that all items

on the agenda were sufficiently covered. This will identify any gaps that may require follow-up and it will give people a positive sense of accomplishment about the meeting.

MAKE SURE THE METTING WAS WORTHWHILE

After the meeting, send out a summary of the meeting including all action items to all the participants and observers and anyone else that requires a copy. Action items should be clearly indicated, with start and completion dates. If follow-up meetings were scheduled, these should also be included.

CASE STUDY

Gemma glanced at the clock on the wall of the meeting room. It was 9:20 a.m. She was the chairperson of the meeting, and it appeared that they were about to go over their allotted time for discussing one of the agenda items.

She addressed the attendees. "While this is an eye-opening discussion we're having about the pros and cons of suggestive-selling, we are about to run over time for this agenda item. Should we end the discussion and move on? Should we continue with the discussion and reduce time for other items? Or would you rather schedule an offline follow-up session? What does everyone think?"

After the participants shared their preferences, it was agreed that they would continue the discussion for five more minutes and reduce the time spent on another topic. This gave deciding power to the participants and kept them on track.

Review

Meetings are necessary for organizations to operate.

- Describe a typical meeting. Does it stay on topic and on time?

- What are some of the reasons that meetings tend to go long and get off track?

- Describe how a good agenda can help manage a meeting.

- Explain how you can split people that attend the meetings into groups. How can this be helpful?

- What is the key to a successful meeting?

11

#10 USE ALTERNATIVES INSTEAD OF MEETINGS

Sometimes, a face-to-face meeting isn't the best solution. In this chapter, we will explore alternatives to meetings that can help you and your team be more productive. Even if you  use a meeting alternative, you should use the PAT approach (p. 58), take minutes, and distribute post-meeting notes and action items.

INSTANT MESSAGING AND CHAT ROOMS

Instant messaging (IM) applications and chat rooms can be a great alternative to meetings, especially if meeting participants are not in the same location.

Keys:

- Use an agenda and stay on task.

- The chairperson's role in keeping things on track is very important.

- Set ground rules at the beginning of the meeting to eliminate distractions such as emoticons, sounds, and acronyms.

- Make sure you keep a record of the meeting.

IM applications:

- WeChat
- WhatsApp
- Facebook Messenger
- Group Me
- Blackberry Messenger
- Tango
- Groups
- Skype
- Campfire
- Meeting Pal

TELECONFRENCING

If more personal contact and real-time sharing is needed, try a teleconferencing system like Adobe's Acrobat.com, Microsoft Live Meeting, or Citrix's GoToMeeting.

Most teleconferencing application features:

- Screen sharing
- Collaboration tools
- Interactive whiteboards
- Voice and text chat
- Meeting recording capabilities (can serve as minutes)

EMAIL LISTS AND ONLINE GROUPS

If your work group needs ongoing, interactive communication, rather than periodic face-to-face meetings, an email list, forum, or online group can be an effective tool.

There are a few options for these online tools. If your organization has the infrastructure in place, you may be able to set something up on site. If they do not have the infrastructure, there are many free tools out there, including Google Groups, Yahoo Groups, and Convos.

Keep in mind:

- A moderator is essential. These types of tools can quickly get out of control without proper management. You will want to make sure members stay on topic and professional.

- Make sure time spent on these tools is monitored to discourage abuse. Setting a daily or weekly update or delivery time may be a good idea.

- Just like meetings, an online list or group should have a purpose and stick to it.

COLLABORATION APPLICATIONS

More sophisticated electronic tools that can reduce the need for meetings are systems like Microsoft SharePoint, Wrike, Pelontonics, Google Docs, and Basecamp can give users interaction and collaboration tools from any location.

These sort of tools may be most beneficial for project meetings, or situations where users need to peer review each other's work. These tools must have a clearly defined, stated purpose and participants must make sure that these time-saving tools do not turn into time wasters.

CASE STUDY

Vivian went to talk with her supervisor, Paul, about her dilemma. When they sat down, Vivian explained, "I wanted to talk to you because I'm just not sure what the best option is for holding a meeting, when there are so many attendees at different locations."

Paul said, "Have you thought about using a chatroom or instant messaging?"

"I didn't think of that," Vivian said. "But won't that make it impossible to stick to an agenda?"

Paul shook his head. "No. It will be more challenging, but not impossible. Let's work on a plan for how you can keep your meeting on track using a chatroom or instant messenger."

Coming up with a plan took only a short period of time. Vivian would have an agenda and make sure to stick to it.

Review

- New applications are being developed every day. Do a Google search for business meeting alternatives and list some options.

- Describe how an application such as google docs can help a team communicate.

- Describe how an IM app can replace a meeting.

- Research the following apps for project and team management:

    o Basecamp

    o Unison

    o Team WorkPM

    o Tello

    o Asana

    o Moovia

    o Storm (Drupal PM)

    o Open Atrium

    o WebCollab

    o Redmine

    o Proof Hub

ABOUT THE AUTHOR

Dr. Jimmy D. Bayes has over twenty-five years working in corporations, nonprofit organizations, and churches.

He has started or helped start four nonprofit organizations and is part owner of a training company.

Training and education has always been his focus and he has an earned Ph.D. in Organizational Leadership from Regent University. He currently conducts training in entrepreneurship, employee training, and organizational development as well as coaching and consulting.

Dr. Bayes lives in Bryan, Texas with his family.

OTHER BOOKS BY AUTHOR

Available on Amazon.com

Do you want to earn more income? Do you want to be your own boss? Do you want more control over your professional life? If you do, then you can start your own business.

Startup Power is a practical guide for starting your own business. "Startup Power" began as a manual for entrepreneur workshops. It has been expanded and now includes a glossary of entrepreneurial terms, an outline for a feasibility study, and an outline for a business plan. This book gives you the information needed to start a new business.

OTHER BOOKS BY AUTHOR

Social groups seek to empower their members, corporations are discovering the benefits of empowering their employees, and organizations seek to empower groups and individuals so that these groups can gain control of their lives and be successful.

Empowerment is categorized as social, structural, or psychological empowerment. This book gives the theoretical background for each aspect of empowerment and lays the foundation for an integrated model of empowerment developed by the author.

The information from this book comes from the author's doctoral research on empowerment. His research found that there is a body of work regarding social, structural, and psychological empowerment, but there are no integrated empowerment models that include all three aspects of empowerment. Additionally, Divine empowerment is addressed and provides the foundation for a four phased integrated empowerment model that includes the social, structural, psychological, and divine aspects of empowerment.

This book is available on Amazon.com

OTHER BOOKS BY AUTHOR

Available on Amazon.com

Disciples of Christ are cleansed by "washing with water through the Word" (Eph. 5:26).

This devotional journal uses the **SOAP Bible Study Method** to study and apply God's Word to the disciple's life.

- **S**cripture
- **O**bservation
- **A**pplication
- **P**rayer

This edition of "Just Add Water" covers Paul's letters of Ephesians, Colossians, and Philemon.

www.ingramcontent.com/pod-product-compliance
Lightning Source LLC
Chambersburg PA
CBHW071329040426
42444CB00009B/2111